Your Best Life Now!

Truly Loving You

&

Writing Your Success Story.

Dr. Alice Besong

Copyright © 2019 Alice Besong. All rights reserved. No part of this book can be reproduced in any form without the written permission of the author and its publisher.

Table of Contents

Dedication 9

Introduction 13

Gratitude From Grief 15

Born To Serve 35

A Compelling Vision 39

Financial stability 45

Visualize It 51

Surround Yourself With Greatness 57

Making Powerful Decisions 63

Make Integrity Your Brand 75

Be Self-Disciplined 77

Choose Faith Over Fear 85

Commit And Take Action. 91

Life Happens FOR Me 97

Conclusion 105

Dedication

To everyone who reads this book: thank you so much for your support!

To Faith and Hope (my two precious daughters): thank you for giving me a STRONG WHY. I love you so much & will keep going to make sure you both have the BEST life.

To mommy Johanna: Thank you for believing in me. Now is the time to rejoice, give thanks, and celebrate. May God continue to bless you & my step-dad, Dr Agborntui, for all that you do.

To Daddy: Mr. Eddy Besong; Thank you for dedicating your entire life to our success. I know your spirit lives on.

To mommy Es: Mrs. Esther Besong: Thank you for laying a strong biblical foundation in my life. May God continue to bless you for all that you do.

To Val & Arah Besong(my borther & sister-in-Law): thank you for being there for me every step of the way. Now is time to celebrate! Val, you are God-sent.

To my aunt: Dr. Alice Taku: Thank you for your unwavering love & support

To uncle Benson Agbortogo (international bestselling author): thank you for inspiring me to write this book and expanding my life's vision.

To Emmanuel & Vicky (my brother & sister-in-law): Thank you so much for all that you do.

To my siblings & other family members including my in-laws:

thank you for your love and support.

To my team at Success Motivation: thank you for helping make my dream come true.

May God continue to bless and reward all of you abundantly.

Introduction

Even as you open the cover of this book, I know because I've been you, you're questioning whether you could truly ever love you. But you want to. You feel driven inside to success, and yet everything outside of you is telling you that success is something you will never have. I'm coming to you to tell you today that success is already yours. That the fulfillment to everything you've ever dreamt of is bottled up, ready to explode from within you.

You truly do not need anything else to be everything you're meant to be. You just need to learn the secret of truly loving you. When you embrace the love for yourself, what you will find pouring out of you is your success story. Today, we are going to begin the process of writing your success story.

Gratitude From Grief

I'm super grateful for the life that I live today. I live every moment of my life in gratitude, happy and fulfilled. The person that I am today goes beyond the person I dreamt of being, to the person I was meant to be. Not because of the things that come to me from the outside world or the material things that I have in my life, but because deep inside of me, I truly know love. I have uncovered about my life and my true purpose. I wake up every morning, excited. I can't wait to see what today is going to bring. What am I going to accomplish today? What amazing thing am I going to be a part of even in the next hour? The excitement of that vision pulls me into each new thing as I delightedly experience it. I live everyday as though it's the best day of my life, because every day I'm alive allows me to create a better version of myself. And I use this better version of me to serve others. To help other people maximize and become all that they can be.

I live by the mantra, "Everything works out for me, and no matter what happens, out of all of this, only good will come." Louise Hay

I approach both the wanted and the unwanted circumstances that come in my daily life, with confidence because I truly believe that everything works out for my good. I see now that it ALWAYS does. All of that stems from the fact that I have truly learned how to love me.

You need to understand, growing up as a little girl, that was not who I was. Even though I was raised in a loving home, as I got older I found myself seeming to always look for love in all the wrong places. I felt like in order to be loved, I needed to find someone out there to love me. I had to look outside for everything. Without that outside love, I couldn't even know what love was.

While in medical school, I met a person. This young man, ironically, had the same last name as me, except with one letter. I will refer to him as Josh, for confidentiality reasons. I fell madly in love with him. In my mind, Josh was God sent, the love of my life, my hero, my knight in shining armor on a white horse, who was going to come, just sweep me off my feet, and we would be married, and life would just be better. I married him and embarked on what was going to be a great life; imagined having children and all of the things that every little girl ever dreams of.

To my great dismay, I had attracted the wrong person into my life. What I didn't know then is that instead of finding my hero, my search for outside love, my search for validation from the things outside of me, had attracted the wrong person into my life. And I ended up, rather than the bliss that I was sure I was going to live in, in disaster.

While preparing to take my medical boards, at home I was constantly being insulted. He always told me that I would never pass my boards. That I would never amount to anything. And honestly, most of the time I believed him. I found myself not doing well on some of my courses because all I could hear was his words resonating in my head. All of this, validating his message. He cheated on me on multiple occasions while I was busy studying for my boards. Robbed me literally, financially. I felt like nothing. How could a young woman like me who was raised with so much love and support, end up in such a toxic relationship?

Don't worry, everything worked out for my good in the end.

I had to pull through and really dig deep into the one thing that always rescued me, which is my faith in God. I had to realize that I had choices. Was I going to stay in a relationship that was not clearly meant to be for me, regardless of what the outside circumstances looked like? Or do I get out of it, file for divorce, lose everything that I had put into it, and start building my life again from scratch while in medical school?

This was tough. But what I discovered was, this wasn't the end, it was only the beginning. And yes, I had to dig really deep. I had to lean heavily into my faith in God and learn that I do have choices. It wasn't easy, but I had to follow my intuition and do what was best for me. I filed for divorce. Walked away; lost all that I had put into it, and started again from scratch. Struggling with my divorce while completing my medical boards, feeling deep shame for filing for divorce, all the while having him continue to tell me that I wasn't worth being a wife. That I'd never become a physician.

I was in a community where you were shamed for filing for divorce. Where you are expected to stay married regardless of the circumstances. Now this same person who mistreated me was going around telling people that I wasn't worth being a wife. That I would never become a physician. I would never amount to anything. I was being insulted in the same community which I was raised in. The same community which knew me as being a fighter and being strong. Even though the people that knew me should have known better, he was now constantly there spreading these vicious lies about me. I had to pull myself through all of that and still have to face those people on a regular basis. I still had to see them on social media or at family gatherings. I pulled myself through all of that.

I'm glad to say that through this storm, I got through. I took my boards. I passed them. Went through my residency, and today I am a physician. Looking back, I am so so happy that I followed my intuition, filed for divorce and moved on with my life. It wasn't easy, but it was VERY worth it.

Learning To Love You

What I had to learn was how to love myself. You see, until we truly learn to love ourselves, we'll never know love. Because true love begins in loving yourself. You can never look outside for the kind of love you need inside. Loving and accepting yourself is the beginning of finding true love.

You attract love to you by becoming a loving person. By becoming love, you attract love. We teach others how to treat us. The kind of love that you deserve, the kind of love that you need, can never come from the outside. Loving you starts and always comes from inside. And loving yourself is the beginning of all the great things you were meant for in life. When you become on the inside, the love that you are and learn to love yourself, then and only then can you attract real love to you.

First, you MUST accept yourself. Know that you are a unique human being who is "perfect in your imperfections."

Embrace all the amazing things about you and acknowledge your weaknesses. Self- awareness allows you to tap into your authentic power. You have to accept who you truly are.

When you really truly love you, you will begin to see love. You will also begin to recognize the wrong kind of love. You will know in advance the people who aren't worthy of the wonderful person that you are, and you will avoid them. But again, the thing to know is that you will never find the love that you deserve, you will never find anyone who will love you more than you love yourself.

Second, you must believe in a higher power; know that you were created to succeed. Do you know of any manufacturer who has ever created a product he or she wants to fail? Think about this for a minute. You were created to succeed along with everybody else on this beautiful planet.

Think about some of the people you admire today. Realize that we were created by the same God, with a unique purpose for each of our lives. We all have the same beginning and end. We all breathe the same air. It's our mission to fulfill the unique purpose within us. You have to know; you were born to succeed.

Next, we have to really spend quality time alone. Be still. Meditate. Connect with the spirit within. It is only from tuning out the outside noise and learning to be still can you begin to know who you are; know what you really want in life and live with intention. In this silence you will hear the most important voice, the ONLY voice that really matters: your intuition, or Inner GPS – God placement system. Only in that stillness will you also receive the love you deserve. If true love is what you want, only by taking the time to truly know and love you, will you ever find true love.

Ask empowering questions....

Ask yourself, "Who am I? What are the things that make me happy?" Not the outside material possessions, but on the inside. What lights me up? What are the thoughts, the attitudes, the actions that truly bring joy into my life? I have discovered that I love, love, love, spending time alone, meditating; time with my girls; volunteering at their school. I enjoy being in nature and dancing. I've even found real love in going to the gym every morning. These things truly make me happy. As we discover what we really love, we learn what really fuels us. Incorporating these things into my daily life has resulted in happiness, peace, and Joy.

Next, have a strong WHY. We need a reason why we MUST have the things we want in life. Not because somebody told us we should have them; not because of some external or materialistic need. Your why must have a deeper meaning. Go for a cause that is way larger than yourself.

A strong why is the most important aspect and is the reason why people achieve success.

Without a strong why, it will be easy to give up when the going gets tough. "If your WHY doesn't make you cry; then your dreams are not big enough." Alice Besong

A strong why will also give your life new meaning. You will wake up every morning knowing that you are doing what you were created to do. You will find joy in everyday life.

Now I thrive when I see people succeed, because I know that I was blessed to be a small part of that success in their lives. Seeing success in others coming from me being able to, in any small way, help them succeed, is the thing that drives me. It's the "why" that wakes me up every morning. It's what gives us the push, and brings joy into our lives.

Also knowing that my daughters, Faith and Hope, will one day read this book and see me thriving, will help them be able to thrive as well. They can find success and be able to keep going in their own lives, no matter what obstacles they will face, as they learn to create a better life for themselves and others.

Knowing that they can see this in me is a wonderful, wonderful gift that I can experience every day.

Born To Serve

We were born to serve. I have realized that we were all born to serve one another and that fulfillment comes from the service and impact we provide.

When we serve others, so many amazing things come back to us.

I remember growing up, my dad used to always make me serve guests. I would be outside playing, or whatever else I was doing. No matter what I was doing, he would make me come in and serve drinks to the guests who were at the house. At first, it really seemed like a chore. It wasn't something that I wanted to do. But then as I began to watch, I began to see the rewards that were coming my way in serving. People telling me, "Thank you." Their lives being better. And as I saw these rewards, learning to serve, became better and better in my life. I love to serve, and do so at every opportunity I'm given now.

The other thing I realized, was the more I served others, the better my life became. You see, we thrive when we serve. Even better, when you love yourself and serve others from a fulfilled state (when your cup runs over), life is AWESOME!

When we serve from a full cup; we can give our BEST in service to others because we're giving to them from the abundant overflow of the love that we have inside of us and our desire to serve and see their lives better. Impact leads to success.

A Compelling Vision

"Whatsoever is true, whatever is noble, whatever is right, whatever is pure, whatever is lovely, whatever is admirable, if anything is excellent or praiseworthy think about such things." Philippians 4:8

"Don't allow your past to cloud the AMAZING vision of your future." Alice Besong

The joy I experience today didn't always come easy at first. Practice makes us better. Today's fulfillment is the result of me working on myself daily and learning to turn every adversity into an opportunity.

I still remember the days when I used to wake up feeling so down because I would only think about the negative things that had happened to me in the past.

I soon realized that "you become what you repeatedly think about." So the sooner I started to focus on the Vision I had for my Life, the better I felt and the more positive and successful experiences I attracted into my life.

"Pain pushes until the Vision PULLs."
Dr Michael Bernard Beckwith

Your pain will keep pushing you down until a compelling vision pulls you out of the situation. When you have circumstances that induce pain, you will always be focused on the painful outcomes and the painful experiences. What I have realized is that creating a compelling vision for my life allows me to have daily routines which have resulted in daily happiness.

ALWAYS have a CLEAR and compelling vision for your life and see painful incidences as an opportunity for growth.

"Happiness is a byproduct of our daily lifestyle choices." **Monk Dandapani**

Do not chase happiness rather create a lifestyle which results in happiness.

Make sure your day is filled with activities which fuel you from the inside and make you happy. I have made it a habit to create these circumstances in my life. They have become such a ritual that I do not depart from them. I still have things that I am working to overcome and get better at. However, I am super grateful and overjoyed to have found self-love, self-fulfillment, peace, and joy.

I feel these are the foundations for creating success and achievement in life.

Financial stability

Financial stability is essential for building a successful life. I can't stress enough how important it is to make sure you have a strong financial base. As a little girl, I knew I wanted to be a doctor and would say so to anyone who was listening, from the time I could speak. Thank God for my parents and family who dedicated their lives to help make my dream a reality.

I moved to the US at age 16 from Cameroon, West Africa (where I was born). My parents spent thousands of dollars towards my education because I did not qualify for loans initially. This taught me to be a responsible, hardworking young lady; lessons I MUST pass down to my daughters, Faith and Hope.

Even with my family's love and support, the journey wasn't easy. However, I am grateful for the hard lessons I had to learn on my own.

I realized that in order for me to grow; in order to have a financially stable life; I would have to work hard. I would have to acquire financial wisdom. I found out the hard way that if you don't learn to save and invest money, you will have financial trouble. If you cannot save and invest a portion of EVERY dollar you earn, then you will not save anything from 40,000 or more. I learned this the hard way.

My hope is to express to you the importance of financial stability. Having a 6 to 12 month emergency fund is a MUST. No matter how much you're earning; your goal should always be to pay yourself first, to invest your money, and never ever live above your means. One time I had to sit and have a deep and honest conversation with myself. During which I said, "Alice if you do not have a budget, track your cash flow regularly, then how do you expect to have money to save and invest at the end of the month?"

"When it comes to financial matters, what you don't know WILL hurt you." Alice Besong

Financial literacy is a must. Studying the basics of investing your earnings, wealth creation and having a prosperity map for your family is a must at every stage of your life. Once you start earning a steady income, please make it your goal to sit down and understand the financial basis for wealth creation. Don't find yourself in a situation where you are living paycheck to paycheck. Statistics show that about 70% of Americans live paycheck to paycheck. It's not about how much you earn but what you do with the money that you earn that really matters. Teachers and dry cleaning business owners make up a large percentage of millionaires in the US. This really goes to show you that it is not how much you earn, but how you spend and invest your money that really matters.

One thing which saved me a great deal of pain, after I started learning the basics of investing my money, was that I stopped buying things I did not need. I stopped spending money on liabilities and started spending money on assets. I realized that buying a good book was definitely an asset as compared to buying something that was just a liability for me. I also realized that unless you own a home which is fully paid off, your home is a liability, NOT an asset.

Visualize It

Everything in life is created twice. First spiritually, then physically. Every creation begins with a thought. Then you imagine what it will feel like to have it. This AWESOME, overwhelming, feeling is what makes you want it. Then your brain starts to figure out ways to help you acquire the thing. From the time we imagine and visualize anything we want to the time of it's physical manifestation we must live by FAITH, not by sight. Without Faith you can very easily give up on your dreams.

So in order for you to be successful at creating anything you want, you must believe in it. You must see it, believe it is possible and know what it will feel like. You must learn to vibrate at the same frequency as what you are creating.

Practice daily visualization. Set aside a few minutes each day during which you close your eyes visualize and feel as if you already have what you want. Nurture that feeling daily until it feels normal to you. Then open your eyes; come back to the present moment, create a plan and start working towards it. This daily practice aligns you spiritually with what you want. This is proof to you that if you can see it in your mind; you will one day hold it in your hand.

In other words, before you have it (physically), you must already have it (spiritually). This fact makes life a little easier for us to understand that there is no dream that we have right now, which cannot be created by us. If God placed a dream within you, then it is possible. You just have to figure out the necessary steps to make it a reality. Daily visualization and feeling is vital.

Visualization alone will not create the urgency and strong pull needed for manifestation. Which is why you must add feelings and practice nurturing those feelings each day.

Your greatest power lies in the present moment so use the present moment to create the life you want to live.

"Consciousness creates reality"
Unknown author

Therefore, we are co-creating our reality intentionally or by default. Choose to create yours intentionally.

Everything you create depends on your present thoughts, visualization, feelings and actions.

As you visualize and create, make sure you enjoy every step of the journey. "Success is a journey, not a destination." **Unknown author**

It is all the little things that we do on a daily basis which add up to make a successful life.

Surround Yourself With Greatness

"You become who you spend time with."– Alice Besong

Surround yourself with the right people. Surround yourself with people who are 20 steps ahead of you. Who will help you reach where you want to go. Surround yourself with people who will see greatness in you even when you cannot see it for yourself. Surround yourself with people who have been in your shoes and have successfully gotten to where you are trying to go and beyond. Surround yourself with positive and optimistic people, who believe in the miracles of life and strive to achieve more and make a difference in the lives of others.

You must understand that life is energy. "Where focus goes, energy flows." Tony Robbins

Anything you focus on will get bigger. So focus on your dreams, not your problems. If you focus on your problems, they will get bigger. If you want your relationships to get better focus and be present with your loved ones. Give them your undivided attention.

If the people you are spending time with are POSITIVE and optimistic, their company will always leave you feeling empowered and encouraged to continue working towards your dreams. If you spend time with TOXIC people you will end up feeling drained and discouraged.

There was a time when I did not feel like my life was heading in the direction that I wanted it to go. My thoughts were not the thoughts or things that I would want to create in my life. After meditating for several months, I realized that I was spending time and listening to a lot of content which did not serve me. I was programming my mind with the news and other content on TV and not really paying attention to the input that came into my brain from my surroundings. After reading a series of books on reprogramming your mind for success, I discovered that reprogramming my mind means being careful with even my close contacts. I started being very selective about what I watched, listened to and especially the people I spent time with.

If you want greatness, you must surround yourself with the right people. If you want to achieve anything, you must surround yourself with people who have achieved that thing and more. You cannot want one thing, spend your time with people who are heading in a different direction, and then blame others for not having what you want in your life. Everyone in life is heading towards a certain direction, whether they know it or not. It's entirely up to you. We have been given the choice to make the decision and be selective about who we spend time with. The sooner we make the decision to spend time with people whom we want to learn from and grow with, the sooner we can steer our lives in the right direction. Know that you are the captain of YOUR ship.

Making Powerful Decisions

"Decisions shape our destiny." Tony Robbins.

The decisions you make today will build or break your tomorrow.

When you learn to love yourself and know your self-worth, have the courage to make life changing decisions.

I still remember right now, decisions that I made that I am so thankful to God that I made them. Those decisions have steered my life in a completely different direction which has served me for the better. Had I not made those decisions and turned the other way, my life would be in a completely different place today.

Thank God, I followed my intuition and made those timely decisions which have now led me down this fulfilling path. My hope and prayer is that as you read this book, you too will learn to follow your intuition and start making decisions that will steer your life in a direction that will bring you more fulfillment and happiness. You too will start living the life of your dreams.

The stories shared in this book are examples from my own life and people I have shared some of my life's experience & worked with so that they too can benefit and hopefully avoid some of the mistakes I made. Their real names are not being used for confidentiality reasons.

Meet Sarah....

Sarah was a very hardworking female physician who was in a relationship with a boyfriend she was hoping would propose to her. As I worked with and got to know her, I could sense her discontent with her current relationship. The more we spoke, I realize that Sarah was just hoping to get married because she was at an age when all her friends were getting married and she felt pressured to do the same. Her current relationship had several red flags and was definitely doomed to be an unhappy union in the future. When Sarah finally asked for my advice; I gave her my opinion and encouraged that she follow her intuition. "Your intuition is your best guide when making decisions," is what I told her. I helped Sarah realize that she could not change a person, her boyfriend, Matt. She could only change herself. "Once you learn to love yourself and know exactly what you want in life, you develop the courage to stand firm to your values. Then, you will attract the right people to you," was my advice to her. Starting a relationship with a random person and hoping that it will work out in the end is a recipe for an UNHAPPY life.

The more we talked the more comfortable she felt and disclosed other issues in the relationship. Sarah later came to the realization that the people she was spending time with right now, including her boyfriend, were not the people she would want to have in her life even a few months from now. Her goal of changing her boyfriend so that his values would reflect her own, was not realistic. He is an adult who has chosen his current life-style. He had been this way his whole life. She could not expect him to change at a moment's notice just because she had known him for about a year or so, was hoping to get engaged and married.

She was setting herself up for a difficult life. A life that would be tedious and would ultimately lead to an unhappy ending.

It was a painful break up for Sarah. But she moved on with her life. After taking some time off relationships to work on herself; She learnt that finding true love begins with you loving yourself. If you cannot make yourself happy, how do you expect someone else to?

With my help; Sarah went through the journey of self-discovery and self-mastery. She learnt that loving yourself makes you a magnet. When you get to the point in life when you can say, "I am enough." You are satisfied and need nothing; you become a magnet and attract everything. Your knowledge of true love is what helps you distinguish the right kind of love from the wrong one.

Sarah later met a more compatible partner who shares her values. Their spiritual partnership has laid the solid foundation for a future filled with love, happiness, and growth.

One thing I realized from doing the inner work on myself and really getting to know who I am is that I now know who to associate with and which people I need to run far away from. There are certain people who, for their own reasons, are heading in a different direction from mine. Not because they are bad people or have anything negative associated with them. It's just that we are not heading in the same direction. Our values and principles do not align. Once I realized this, I had to start making the decision to find people who are more in tune and aligned with my goals and my direction in life. People that I could learn from, and also contribute to their success. Having a coach who is 20 steps ahead of me was one of such great moves.

When you learn to love yourself and have a clear vision for your life, your vision dictates who you spend time with and who you allow to influence you. Until you have a clear vision for where your life is going and who/what you want to attract into your life, you'll leave the people you meet to chance. Don't gamble with your future. You will allow people who should not be in your life to influence you, and people who are not necessarily aligned with your values to influence you.

Have the courage to make powerful life-changing decisions, NO MATTER WHAT. Life is a journey, not a destination and there will be people you have to let go in order to make room for others. This includes family, friends, and even a spouse. Have the courage to let them go, gracefully, and move on. Know that when your values no longer ALIGN with a close contact, something MUST change. Do

NOT compromise on your values or INTEGRITY for anyone.

Make Integrity Your Brand

Integrity breathes success.

Remember, "whatsoever you do to the least on my brothers; that you do unto me." We are all ONE. The energy you give out always comes back to you, usually multiplied. ALWAYS do the RIGHT thing ... NO MATTER WHAT.

Make integrity and excellence your brand.

When you help others succeed, you too will thrive. The law of compensation, also known as the law of sowing and reaping, states that "each person is compensated in like manner for which he or she has contributed." **Ralph Waldo Emerson.** Therefore, we will be rewarded according to the service we provide to others.

Give your best at all times. Be willing to contribute 100%, over deliver and be transparent every step of the way. Loving yourself helps you become the BEST version of yourself so you can give your BEST service to the world.

Be Self-Disciplined

Make self-discipline your best friend. We all have 24 hours a day. Our energy is a very scarce resource. However, with self-discipline, you can buy back time. You can have time for the most important things in your life. Prioritize your day. Do what matters first thing in the morning before your day gets hijacked. After studying the habits of highly successful people, I have realized that they procrastinate on less important tasks and focus on the most important things of the day. Having a clear vision for your life and being self-disciplined will allow you to work on your goals on a daily basis.

Focus on one thing at a time. If your goals seem too big right now; you are on the right track. Next, break your goals down into bite-size pieces. Then you will realize that it is something doable. Work on your goals EVERY SINGLE DAY to accomplish 1 to 3 tasks needed to move you forward.

Celebrate every small win, as this gives you the momentum to keep going. This is the key to accomplishing your goals and living a successful life.

Meet Chris

I once worked with a nurse named Chris, who had such a hard time prioritizing her activities and getting her work done. She did not realize that spending time on less important tasks was taking her away from fulfilling her goals as a full-time nurse and PHD student. After sitting down with her and going through her entire day's activities, she realized how much time was being wasted throughout her day. She was doing things randomly. Focusing on activities that really didn't matter. She eventually learned to work with a calendar, instead of having a long to do list. As a result of prioritizing her activities she was able to complete the most important tasks on a daily basis. Moving her forward towards accomplishing her goals.

Your time and energy are valuable assets. Focusing your energy and time on activities that really matter will bring you the greatest return in life. This is the key to success. We all have 30 things that we would like to do in one day. However, studies have shown that only a couple of those things will move you forward and get you going in the direction of success.

This was a huge struggle for me when I first started this journey of personal growth and development. I was a jack of all trades. I had no priorities and was ready to do 50 things at once.

Understanding that achieving success in life means prioritizing the most important activities and really doing only what matters on a daily basis brought a whole new perspective to me. Applying this principle has dramatically changed my life.

As a result, I enjoy my responsibilities of being a mother to 2 beautiful girls, a full-time physician, a speaker, author and CEO of Success Motivation. By the time this book hits the shelf we have released our first online course. This will be the first of many courses at our online SUCCESS UNIVERSITY. I am super excited. I enjoy what I do every single day because I have mastered self-discipline.

I now choose one to three things which I do on a daily basis, first thing in the morning, before attending to any other activity in life. Because these things are what will move me forward and closer to accomplishing my life's vision.

To stay motivated, I stick to a positive and empowering daily morning and bedtime routine.

Before going to bed at night, I write down 5 things, which occurred during the day, that I am grateful for in my gratitude journal. A practice I learned from Oprah Winfrey. This ritual has improved my happiness and helps me keep things in perspective.

Having self-discipline not only helps you have more time for the things that are really important in life but also allows you to prioritize your time. Self-discipline also gives you more energy to devote to the things that really matter because you can only do so many things in one day. Your ability to focus and get things done will contribute to your self-confidence and success.

Choose Faith Over Fear

Face your fears. When I realized that everyone else had fears and that fear is an illusion, I decided to face my fears head on. I also had no choice but to become fearless when I went through a near-death experience. I realize that our experiences in life are meant to bring us closer to the person we were meant to be. Whether it is something you regard as being good or bad, the result of these experiences is who you become. If who you become is the best and truest version of yourself, then it's a win-win. Become fearless in ALL your endeavors

The choice of choosing faith over fear also comes easier when we reflect on our accomplishments. Reflect on the things throughout our lives, those tiny accomplishments we were able to do just by proceeding with faith and not letting fear stop us. Most times, when we have a choice, we choose fear and stop short of our goals. However, when we are forced to face circumstances which we have no choice but to face, we go through them and succeed. We realize that fear was just a minor part of our success. I have truly learned that having faith is a vital key to success.

I now use faith instead of fear to encourage my patients diagnosed with a terminal disease. I ask them to imagine and start living the kind of life they would want if they were suddenly disease-free.

"Who would you spend more time with? How would you enjoy your life? Would you want to attend your son's or daughter's graduation?" Are a few of the exciting scenarios I introduce to get them focused on enjoying life.

"Faith is the oil which keeps the machine of life running smooth."

Let faith fuel you.

If you focus on fear and are worried about the outcome of anything in life, then you create anxiety and invite unwanted events into your life. However, when you focus on Faith, you literally live life knowing that everything works out for your good.

One thing I have also realized in my own life, is that faith builds faith and fear builds fear. So when facing any situation, having even a little bit of faith in the beginning, helps you build more faith as you go and grow through the situation. When faced with any situation, I know I will succeed or learn a lesson. So I see every event in life as either a blessing or a lesson. The lessons ultimately, become blessings.

Start with the smallest amount of faith possible. It always helps to know someone else who has gone through what you are going through so that you are empowered and encouraged to succeed. My hope is to be that person to others. Let me be that person for you. Let me be that person who allows you to know that when you go through a near-death experience, you'll come out, thrive and be a better person than before. Let me be that one person who allows you to go through a troubled marriage and come out knowing that you too can succeed. Let me be that person who allows you to know that you can start from scratch, go through school, succeed and be prosperous. Let me be that person who is your example, the person who lets you know that when you have faith and believe, ALL things are possible.

Commit And Take Action.

Take inspired action, action, action, action, towards your dreams and goals.

Do the work.

Success will not happen unless you take consistent action. "Faith without works is dead." Make sure you take action every single day to accomplish what you want in life. Know what you want, plan and take action. Small action steps every single day will create a successful journey.

"Urgency creates relevancy." Benson Agbortogo (international best-selling author).

Have daily goals, weekly goals, monthly goals & yearly goals and work with a sense of urgency towards accomplishing each goal.

Most times we want to move a huge mountain in one day. That usually doesn't happen.

This was a huge lesson I learned from one of my favorite coaches. Creating bite-sized goals which you can do every single day is the key to a successful goal being accomplished. If the task seems too big right now it is because you have not chopped it into smaller pieces. Make sure you can break down your goal, whatever it is you want to accomplish, into something that you can do every single day. For example, writing a book. You cannot sit down in one sitting and write an entire book; however, if you set a doable goal of writing one paragraph every day, then before you know it, you will have an entire book.

Patience is a virtue. Be patient with yourself. Everything in nature happens patiently and slowly. Know that your dreams and goals will come true provided you take inspired action and practice patience. It is the lack of patience, which causes people to compromise on their principles and integrity. Most people want it, and they want NOW. Forgetting that the abundance which surrounds us was created patiently and slowly.

The spiritual evidence of your success will proceed it's physical manifestation. When you start noticing this change, REJOICE and give thanks. This is evidence that your are on the right path.

Taking daily action ensures that you are doing your part and leaving the rest up to God to make it happen for you. Do not compromise on your standards. Do not take advantage of people who have less knowledge than you do. Do not do what is against what your belief for the sake of money. Proceed patiently, with integrity and confidence, knowing that you ARE success and therefore MUST succeed.

Life Happens FOR Me

The foundation of my success stems from the fact that I truly believe that "Life happens FOR me." Not TO or AGAINST me. I know that ALL things work out for my good, no matter what comes my way. For many of us, the events of life have brought us down. We lack the self-confidence needed to press on. Often, because we've based our confidence on all the outside things around us. But we have to learn that the outside world should not be the basis for what we determine is who we are and should definitely never be how we truly love ourselves. As you learn who you truly are and begin to see the spiritual part of you; the divine within; the God force inside of you, then you can begin to be the amazing soul you were created to be. You can look at others who have succeeded, and know with confidence that you too were created for success.

Knowing this amazing creation that God created in me, is the foundation for the unshakable self-confidence required for success. This is the origin of self-love.

When we base our confidence on things from the outside; when those things change, our confidence changes. But when we love ourselves from the inside, and align with the spirit within us, then we have true self-confidence. You literally become unstoppable.

In life you have to sometimes get what you do NOT want to know what you want. If you feel unhappy right now, that's really a good sign. It's a sign that you're not where you should be, and it's a warning sign for you to begin to take that journey towards truly loving yourself.

Get to know you. Find out what makes you happy. Write down the non-materialistic things you want in life: true love, peace, joy, happiness...

Who do you want to be? What kind of work do you enjoy doing? Who are you meant to serve? Be specific. Write these things down vividly so that you can visualize yourself being this person. Only through having these things written down clearly and being able to visualize and feel as if you already have them, will you be able to manifest them into your life. Anything we want in life is desired because we feel it will make us happy. Ask yourself what it would feel like to live your dream life right now. Then choose to live in this happy state every day; No matter what.

Words are powerful. Know that your words are powerful and begin to speak your success into existence.

"..so My word that proceeds from My mouth will not return to Me empty, but it will accomplish what I please, and it will prosper where I send it."
Isaiah 55:11

My encouragement to you today is to adopt a few things that you're going to say about yourself every day.

The two mantras that I would suggest you print out, put on your wall and say to yourself over and over until you know that it's true. First, "Everything works out for me." Say this over & over. Multiple times a day. "Everything works out for me." Then, I want you to say to yourself, "Life happens FOR me." So often we live in a space where life happens to us, but now I want you to have as your mantra, that you say to yourself over and over again, "Life happens FOR me." Know that this is true. Know that life happens for you. Believing this will allow you to turn every adversity in life, into an opportunity.

Lastly, I give you this affirmation for truly loving yourself. Practice this one in front of a mirror daily. "I love and accept myself for who I am." Say it over and over. Affirm it in your own life. "I love and accept myself for who I am." As you write down vivid visualizations of who you are, as you speak these mantras and affirmations over your life, you are writing the success story of your life.

Conclusion

You are being and becoming the person you are meant to be. Your success story is there, it's within you. It comes from you truly loving you. I can't wait to hear your success story. I can't wait to see you truly loving you. I am excited to see you live out every day of your life in a powerful, passionate way, as you go from joy to joy, love to love, success to success, while you're writing your success story.

www.ingramcontent.com/pod-product-compliance
Lightning Source LLC
Chambersburg PA
CBHW070802220526
45466CB00002B/517